Hello, My Friend

Hello, My Friend

Linda Byrne O'Riordan

Pearly Gates Publishing LLC™, Houston, Texas (USA)

Copyright © 2017
Linda Byrne O'Riordan

All Rights Reserved.
No portion of this publication may be reproduced, stored in any electronic system, or transmitted in any form or by any means (electronic, mechanical, photocopy, recording, or otherwise) without written permission from the publisher. Brief quotations may be used in literary reviews.

ISBN 13: 978-1945117572
ISBN 10: 1945117575
Library of Congress Control Number: 2017931907

For information, contact:
Pearly Gates Publishing LLC™
Angela Edwards, CEO
P.O. Box 62287
Houston, TX 77205
BestSeller@PearlyGatesPublishing.com

Hello, My Friend

Dedication

This book is dedicated to all the men, women, young men, and young women who have lost their lives to suicide - and to their partners, families, and friends.

This is also dedicated to **YOU** - the reader.

I encourage you to hold on:

The dawning of a new day awaits you.

Hello, My Friend

Acknowledgements

This book was written with you - the reader - in mind. Whether you are a mother, father, partner, sister, brother, niece, nephew, cousin, or friend who has lost someone to suicide **or** you are someone who is at a very low place in life and have been contemplating ending your own life, **please know that you are not alone**…no matter what category of person you are from the list of people I just mentioned.

There are others who were in the same position you are in today. They, too, once felt all alone in their plight - just as you are feeling right now. Were it not for the love and support of others, including the relevant support services available, they would not have made it through that dark tunnel. Reach out to and meet others who are in the same position as you are in at this moment.

Begin your journey of coming out of the darkness.

I offer much love and encouragement to you on your road to recovery.

~ Linda

Hello, My Friend

Introduction

I began writing *Hello, My Friend* on January 3, 2017. Two days later, it was complete. I can only describe the experience as a spiritual encounter - one that I had on New Year's Eve of 2016.

I had been **eagerly** awaiting the turn of the New Year to see the release of another book I had spent many months working on. After the spiritual encounter on New Year's Eve, I decided it was not the time for me to release that book, but rather this one.

Sometimes in life, we make plans. Then, God intervenes and leads us in the direction we are supposed to go. *I guess that is what happened to me.*

When most people were ringing in the New Year, I was at home reflecting on the family, friends, and other people who had lost loved-ones to suicide. In **that** moment, I thought about how the ringing in of the 'new' and closing of the 'old' would be a rather sad time *(as opposed to happy)* for them - myself included.

Hello, My Friend

My life's story includes the loss of my **very** best friend to suicide many years ago. I know he would have wanted me to write something that would touch others who may be contemplating taking their own lives - a message of hope for the future and, at the same time, to comfort those who have lost loved-ones.

As I typed **every word**, I felt I was being inspired and led.

My prayer is that this book will help and comfort each reader as they apply the contents to wherever they may be in their own lives.

Hello, My Friend
Preface

The story you are about to read is one of a young man I encountered one day at a funeral I attended. In fact, it was **HIS** funeral. "*His funeral?*" you may ask. Yes: His own funeral.

You may find that hard to believe *(and I cannot say I would blame you)*, but I hope by the time you reach the end of this story, you will be a believer.

I was standing in the distance paying my respects. The man they were laying to rest often bought me food and gave me money when he was alive. You see, I am a homeless man and had lived on the streets of the same town that young man lived in for many years. He was one of the many people who had shown me kindness in my time there. I received the news that he had taken his own life, and it saddened me because he had always been such a happy-go-lucky kind of guy in all the time I had known him.

I suppose no one really knows what goes on in the mind of others…

Anyway, I will let **you** read the story and shall return later in the Conclusion of this book.

Hello, My Friend

TABLE OF CONTENTS

DEDICATION VI

ACKNOWLEDGEMENTS VII

INTRODUCTION VIII

PREFACE X

THE STORY OF 'MY LIFE' 1

CONCLUSION BY THE "HOMELESS MAN" 42

SUPPORT SERVICES IN

CLONMEL, COUNTY TIPPERARY, IRELAND 45

Hello, My Friend

Hello, My Friend
The Story of 'My Life'

The night I took my life, I had been drinking. In fact, for a few days prior to my death, I had been drinking. I used to drink to escape reality and have fun, but the next day would always leave me feeling depressed and alone. Even when I was in the company of other people, I quite often felt all alone.

I had **one** friend who understood me…to a degree. I now see she only understood me to the degree in which I was prepared to reveal myself to her. She knew when I would be feeling down on myself and, to be honest, she saved me from a few suicide attempts in the years we had been friends. I could open up to her in ways I found difficult to open up to others, yet I never really ***FULLY*** told her how I was feeling. Sometimes, I would look at her and want to tell it all, as I knew she loved me dearly - but she had many troubles of her own and I didn't want to add to them. In hindsight, I wish I had been more honest with her because after I died, she was the one who discovered my body. To see the effects it had on her left me **devastated**, as I would never have hurt her. **EVER.**

Hello, My Friend

I watched her for the following few years after my death. She was trying to hold herself together for her children and attempting to get on with everyday life, but it was **so** hard for her. She cried many nights, all the while blaming herself for "*not seeing it coming*". She was left wondering if she had been as good a friend as she believed she was to me.

The answer to that is "YES!"

She was a **good** friend. She was there for me at *all* times. No matter what time of day or night, when I needed her, she was there. She now lives with the feeling of having let me down. That is so far from the truth.

Hello, My Friend

You see, I should have been honest with her and told her about how I was feeling. She would have helped me receive the help I so needed - as others would have, too - had I told them how I was feeling. I was ashamed to reach out because I was afraid of being classified as '*weak*' or '*vulnerable*'. I was **never** going to portray myself as either. *How could I? What would people think of me if I admitted I was broken inside and needed help?* I was, after all, the "Happy-Go-Lucky Joker" who had it all (in other people's eyes): a partner, beautiful children, a lovely home, a good job, and **lots** of friends. I was not going to let **anyone** believe I was **'weak'.**

All of that was, of course, a **lie**. I now know that reaching out for help is *exactly* what I should have done. In fact, it is a sign of **strength** to ask for help when you are feeling low - not a weakness like I led myself to believe at the time. In reality, it takes a lot of courage to admit to others that you are feeling bad inside.

Weakness is actually absent in the search for help. Strength and courage are revealed in three simple words:

I NEED HELP.

Hello, My Friend

Those words have a *strong* effect on the human emotion, much like the words "*I love you*" coming from the person you have always longed to hear them from. That feeling you have when hearing those words are the **same** feelings you have when you say ***"I need help"*** to the right professionals or personal friend. You may not believe that right now, but I am telling you the truth: **When those words are spoken, it is the start of recovery for you.**

• • • • •

Hello, My Friend

I am not going to go into my whole life's story or the events that led up to me taking my own life; rather, I am going to focus on how I **felt** that night...

I was alone in my house after having returned from having a few drinks. As the night bore on and I started sobering up, I started to feel the pain rise inside of me. My mind was numb. It was like there was a hole in my very being that nothing nor no one could fill. I began to think of my children and partner - and how they would be better off without me. In fact, my whole **family** would have been better off. Those were the thoughts I had, given the mindset I was in at the time.

Little did I know: When they found out about my death, it began a downward spiral for all of them - **NOT** the relief I had convinced myself my being gone would have been for them.

I watched my partner fall apart as she tried to explain to our children that I was now in Heaven. With tears in her eyes and an indescribable pain in her heart, my children looked at her while trying to understand: ***I was*** **never** *coming back.*

Hello, My Friend

I watched my family and friends go through life blaming themselves for what happened to me and, at times, blaming each other. They thought it had something to do with what they may have said or done to me. It wasn't. It was something I felt *outside* of my family and friends. It was a gaping hole in my heart and a belief that I was unworthy and worthless. I was *sure* the way I was feeling, **no one** had ever felt and would **never** understand if I were to try to explain. Even in this moment, I cannot think of the words to match or justify the way I felt. It was like there were no words in the **entire** English vocabulary to describe the emptiness I had inside.

I just sat there with tears running down my face as I revisited old and present places - ones that seemed to hold no answer. I reached the conclusion that the only way to end the pain once and for all was to end it all...***permanently***.

I now know that was all a lie, too, that my pain was breeding into my thoughts and emotions. There was a way, and I want to tell you **right now** that if you are feeling *anything* like I did that night, I promise you: **If you hold on for one more day and read my story through to the end, you *will* discover that way.**

• • • • •

Hello, My Friend

I was sitting on the side of my bed. I had written a letter to my loved-ones and put my affairs into place…then, I took my life.

My next memory is of me looking down and seeing my lifeless body. From where I was, I could see a man who didn't **really** want to die, but he was hurting and could not find the strength to reach out for help.

Within what felt like *seconds*, my friend entered my home and found my lifeless body. I now know it was (in fact) a few **days** after I had taken my life, but where I am now, there is no concept of time: *It literally felt like **seconds** had passed.* I watched her as she screamed and ran from my home out into the street. Her son (who had come with her) cried at the sight of his mother pulling her hair out and screaming through the tears falling from her eyes. She tried to compose herself when my partner rang her as she told my partner, *"No; I haven't seen him yet"* - as she didn't want to tell her I had died. She didn't know **how** to tell her, so she said nothing of my death at that time. I watched my friend as she rang the police. Even then, she could not find the words to tell them what happened to me.

Hello, My Friend

Within an hour, everyone had arrived on the scene and gathered outside at my front gate in shock and disbelief. I went from face to face and could see the pain in each set of eyes as they tried to take in all that had unfolded. I found I could genuinely look into each of their hearts, and what I saw was a great love for me that I had thought was not there. I could now see it was my pain that had me thinking the opposite. I could **see** their memories as they thought back to the last time each had seen me. I could **feel** their wishes that they could have known how I was feeling - but how could they? I had **always** put on a brave face around everyone, yet there they were; each taking responsibility in their own way for what I had done without saying so to each other.

I tried to shout at them, **"NO! IT IS NOT ANYONE'S FAULT!"**, but it was useless. They could not hear me. Instead, they all stared blankly at my front door waiting for my body to be removed.

They remained gathered at my gate for a couple of hours and said a few prayers. They were then advised to go to their homes and told they would be contacted in the morning.

Hello, My Friend

I watched as they all entered their cars and drove away slowly and brokenhearted.

My partner went home to our children. I watched her sit up **all** night smoking cigarette after cigarette and looking off into space in total shock.

• • • • •

Hello, My Friend

I entered the room where my friend who found me was sitting. Her children were asleep and she sat staring out the bedroom window thinking back to what she had just witnessed. The trauma of discovering I had passed away and would never return caused a flood of tears to flow down her face.

I spent the rest of that night sitting and watching my partner try to piece together in her head and heart what just happened. She wished it was all a bad dream, but she knew it wasn't. I heard her as she spoke aloud asking me, *"What should I do now? How will I go on?"* Then, she broke down, fell to her knees, and said, *"You probably cannot even hear me"*. I went to her and put my arms around her while rubbing her head, but there was no use. She could neither see nor hear me.

Right then and there, I **knew** I had made the wrong decision. I wanted to turn back time, but I couldn't.

The coming days were filled with my partner, family, and friends trying to organize my funeral and, at the same time, deal with the pain of suddenly losing me.

Hello, My Friend

At my funeral service, my friend (whom I always loved to hear sing) sang in the church - but it was **very** hard for her. I watched as she held the railings and asked God to give her the strength to sing without breaking down. I gently placed my hand on hers and watched her sing from her heart for me. She also sang an Irish song at my graveside as my body was lowered into the ground.

Hundreds of people showed up for my funeral. As I did before, I went from person to person and could see each of their memories regarding me. I saw reflections of the time I spent with each of them and the joy I brought to their lives at different times down through the years. I began to feel the joy they had brought to my life…moments I had **completely** forgotten about.

Hello, My Friend

There was a childhood friend of mine there. He was my best friend when we were children. We used to get into all sorts of mischief. I could see he was thinking back to when we were 10 years old and had stolen walkie-talkies out of a van belonging to a gas company. He went to one end of the football field on our estate and I went to the other end. We talked back and forth on those walkie-talkies. Later that evening, after returning to our own homes, he radioed me saying, *"Breaker! Breaker! Will you bring some potatoes down to my house? We are out of them."* With that, a man's voice broke through and said, **"Give back the walkie-talkies now, you two!"** Much like children would do, we were laughing at and mocking the man while having some innocent fun. Tears rolled down my face as I recalled that memory and countless others we made with each other down through the years.

His thoughts then went to him asking questions like, *"Was I not there enough for him? Why didn't he reach out to me?"* The answer to those questions is simple: My friend also had his own wife and family. I didn't want to bother him with **my** problems. Looking at him at my funeral, I knew he dearly loved me. I should have reached out to him, as I know he would have been there for me.

Hello, My Friend

As I walked away from him with a heaviness in my heart, I saw his sisters who I also grew up with. They were both lost in their own thoughts of the memories we made together down through the years. I also saw people I had worked with - and still others I had forgotten about over time. They, too, were all thinking back to the memories we made. In fact, the whole graveyard seemed to be like a large cinema with **hundreds** of screens. On each screen were memories of me. I never realized the impact my life had on so many people and the joy I had brought to their lives. It took me dying and attending my own funeral to see that, but looking back, I could see all of those happy memoires were buried within me, too - had I looked deep enough. However, my sadness prevented me from doing so.

The priest spoke a few words while all of that was going on, but hardly anyone was listening. They were lost in their own thoughts. And me? Well, I continued to walk from person to person, looking into their eyes and knowing that the memories each had would be their last of me. I was not going to be around to make any other memories, and that saddened me deeply.

Hello, My Friend

Once the burial service was over, everyone left one by one. I was left alone looking at my grave. **AGAIN**, I regretted what I had done and wished I could go back to that night and change *everything*.

• • • • •

Hello, My Friend

After some time, I could see a man in the distance. He was beckoning me to approach him - or so I thought. I looked behind me just in case he was directing his attention at someone else, but no; it was me. I thought to myself, "*This person can see me!*" I walked towards him, all the while feeling a bit excited. If I am really honest, because I had not spoken to anyone in days, the thought of being able to interact with someone was relieving! The closer I got to him, I could see it was a homeless man who lived in our town. I asked him, "*How can you see me?*" He replied, "*I have always seen you.*"

I thought to myself, **"A smartass if I ever seen or heard one!"**

I continued: "*No, I mean I am dead. You do know that was **my** funeral that had just taken place? No one else can see nor hear me anymore, but strangely, you can. I was just wondering: How that can be so?*"

He looked at me, smiled, and replied rather sarcastically, "*So, you have just been to your own funeral? That's a bit Irish now, isn't it? But I suppose had I not seen it with my own two eyes, I wouldn't have believed it. Then again, they do say believe nothing you see and only half of what you hear!*"

Hello, My Friend

I looked at this man who, I might add, I had often given some money and food to from time to time down through the years. I realized in that moment: In **all** the years I had seen him in my hometown, I *never* knew his name. He was always referred to as 'The Homeless Man'. It began to dawn on me that he was going through life in my hometown without a true identity. I asked him, *"What is your name, anyway? I just remembered I never asked you that before."* He replied, *"Ah, just call me 'My Friend'. That's what most people who take the time to notice me call me when they show me some charity in the giving of food or money. They usually say, 'Now, 'My Friend', that is for you', while they hand me whatever it is they choose to."*

*"Okay. So, 'My Friend', can you tell me what is going on here? Have you died, too? Where is **YOUR** grave?"* I asked.

He replied, *"I cannot tell you **WHAT** is going on, but I can tell you what **WOULD HAVE** happened had you not decided to end your own life."*

I was kind of angered by his reply and responded in an angry tone, **"Oh, can you now? Well, then: WHAT would have happened?"**

Hello, My Friend

Again, he just smiled at me and said, "*Follow me.*" When he spoke those two words, I was **immediately** taken back to the night I ended my life, but the man was nowhere in sight. I had no memory of me having died or what transpired after it. It was just me on that night with all the feelings I felt, but this time, instead of ending my life, I just climbed into bed and fell asleep. I was feeling very sad and low.

I woke the following morning to my phone ringing. It was my friend - the girl who had found my body. She was all excited as she told me about being accepted for a course she had applied for and that she was settling into her new home. She asked me what day I was coming down to see her with my partner and children.

Hello, My Friend

You see, earlier in the night before I ended my life, I spoke to her and said I was calling to see her with my family in a few days. I never gave **any** indication I was not going to be around. I told her we would come the following day. We spoke for a few more minutes and, if I'm honest, we had a good laugh on the phone - just as we always did. Both of us had a way of turning any situation we were in into something funny. We had a way of seeing the funny side of things that others might not have been able to see. I loved her for that. We ended our conversation by saying we would speak the next day - like we **always** did.

Hello, My Friend

I then rang my partner.

My partner and I planned a day out with the children, so I headed down to our family home and started to get the children ready. I was still a bit down on myself but chose to put it at the back of my mind and have a good day with my family - which I did. We had **great** fun and the children really enjoyed themselves. When we arrived home, the children were exhausted. We fed, bathed, and put them to bed. My partner and I sat down together that night and watched a film. Then, we went to bed and fell asleep in each other's arms.

The next day, we headed down to my friend's house like I had promised. We also had a good day! While I was there, my cousin rang me. I had also planned to meet up with her the following night for a night out. We ended our phone call while laughing at something that happened within our extended family - yet **WE** were getting the blame for it. My cousin and I were always getting up to all sorts.

Hello, My Friend

The evening wore on and the time came to head home. My partner and I put the children in the car and drove home. On our drive, my cousin rang again to tell me the police had been at my grandmother's over an incident that happened with a neighbor and that the aunt of the friend I had just left was involved. She went on to say my grandmother was all worked up about it. My cousin asked me to call and see my grandmother when I made it back to town. I said I would. I then rang my friend to tell her and she told me she had just heard about it right after I left her home. Again, we just made fun out of it and couldn't wait to find out the *whole* story.

My partner just looked at me and said, "*What are the two of you like; laughing at something like this?*" She didn't understand our laughter is what kept us going. Remember: I said we had a way of turning **everything** into something funny, no matter the situation. After briefly explaining that, I could see her snigger to herself as she looked out the passenger window of the car trying to hide her reaction. I nudged her to let her know I had seen her laugh - and both of us burst into laughter.

Hello, My Friend

When we arrived home, there was a letter in the hall addressed to me. The letter contained some **very** good news I had been waiting on. I was delighted! My partner and I laughed and jumped around after reading the good news!

It was dated the exact day I actually took my own life.

• • • • •

Hello, My Friend

In an **instant**, I was back in the graveyard with 'My Friend'. I asked him about what just happened, and he explained I was given just a *glimpse* of the preceding 48 hours of my life - had I **NOT** taken my own life.

He went on to say that next, we were going to have a look into the lives of those affected by my suicide.

He explained the time was one year after my death. I asked, "*How could that be so when I had just literally attended my own funeral minutes before I met you?*"

He said to me, "*Son, time is nothing in the realm in which you exist now. A day is a thousand years and a thousand years is a day…*"

We walked out of the cemetery and, as we strolled, I asked him how he had come to be homeless. He told me he was not always the way he is now and that in his younger days, he was a carpenter by trade. He said his stepdad trained him and when he came to be in his 30s, he became a revolutionist. I jokingly said to him, "*You were a child of the 60s?*" He laughed and said, "*Yes; I have seen and lived through that era, too.*"

Hello, My Friend

He further explained that one day, he woke up and realized that being a carpenter was not his **true** calling. He had grown sick of seeing the way the government and authorities were treating people. He left home to begin his journey of becoming a revolutionist. He said he became homeless *instantly* - the very **second** he left his parents. After a week or so, he started to recruit others who, along with him, rebelled against the authorities and all they stood for in those days. They would go from town to town standing in the streets, calling for followers who would also join their fight against all the bad things that were taking place across the country and, after a while, they had **thousands** of followers.

Hello, My Friend

I asked him what the government thought of them and did they try to stop them. He said they saw him as a threat and, on many occasions, tried to shut him up. They had no idea how to *effectively* stop them because all the authorities knew was violence - and he and his followers stood for love and peace. That, of course, was something alien and new to the authorities because all they had **ever** known was violence and hate, so they could not come up with a strategy to stop the revolution without angering the people. Reacting in a violent manner would have caused an even ***greater*** uprising in the district…and they did not want that.

I replied, "'My Friend', *you were a hippie; yes?*" Again, he laughed and said, "*You could say that. Yes. I was the **first** hippie!*"

As we were ending that conversation, it was then I realized we had walked to the housing estate where I had grown up. We were standing opposite the field where I used to play as a child. There were children there running around and playing games.

Hello, My Friend

He turned to me and said, "*The innocence of children, eh?*" I agreed with him. He then said, "*None of them know what life holds for them in the future as they grow. They don't worry about **anything**. In fact, they don't look beyond where they are **RIGHT NOW** at this moment in time, do they? They **LITERALLY** live in the moment - from minute to minute, hour to hour, day to day, month to month, and year to year. Somehow, they seem to bounce back from any falls or bruises they get from playing their lives out as they go through childhood. They continue to smile and play without dwelling on yesterday's falls and bruises or even thinking about tomorrow's falls and bruises.*" Again, I agreed with him. He went on: "*If only we, as adults, could look at life through the eyes of children and enjoy where we are **RIGHT NOW** instead of fretting over the future or dwelling on past hurts, maybe we, too, could smile.*"

Hello, My Friend

I stood there and pondered over what he just said. He was right: If, as adults, we could just live in the "here and now" and not allow the past to interfere with our 'right now' or look too far into the future with worry about what **MIGHT** happen down the line, maybe then we could be happy 'for now'. Every minute, every hour, every day, every month, and every year would eventually all add up to a life lived in the **'RIGHT NOW'**, dealing only with every worry in the moment in time it was presented - rather than bringing that past worry into our future or living a worry that has yet to happen by allowing our thoughts to dwell on the "what ifs". Yes. I had to agree with him. A life lived in the **'RIGHT NOW'** sounded much easier than trying to live a life dealing with past issues and issues that have not even been presented in an unknown future.

Hey! I *(above anyone living)* know that none of us are guaranteed the future **or** its worries, so again: **A life lived in the present is a lot easier!**

• • • • •

Hello, My Friend

In the distance, I could hear children singing 'Happy Birthday'. I turned around and immediately noticed I was now standing in the kitchen of my partner's home. Nothing looked at all familiar. I asked 'My Friend' why that was, and he informed me that she had moved away after my death to try to piece back together her life and those of our children. I felt quite saddened by this revelation. I could see my children, partner, and a few close friends gathered around the table singing 'Happy Birthday' to my son. He had gotten so big! 'My Friend' told me it was his fifth birthday. I looked at him in shock and said, "*My son was coming up on his one-year-old birthday when I died, and now it was his **FIFTH** birthday?*" Again, he reminded me there is no concept of time in the realm in which I now existed.

Hello, My Friend

My son was so like me; the spitting image, actually. I had to smile as I watched him blow out his candles and make his wish. My smile soon disappeared when I heard his wish through his thoughts: "*I wish for my Daddy to come home.*" I rubbed his head and whispered into his ear, "*I am here, son*" - but just like with all the others, he could not see me, hear me, nor feel my touch. My partner approached him and held him close to her as if she, too, had seen inside his mind and knew what he wished for. I suppose being a mother, she could sense his desire…the way only mothers can.

The tears welled up in her eyes as she tried to be happy for our son and everyone else who was there. Through her tears, she managed a smile. As I looked into her **VERY** being, I could see how broken her heart truly was.

At this stage, I was truly *(if not **MORE** than before)* regretting having died and leaving my family.

Oh, if only I could have turned back time and changed everything…

• • • • •

Hello, My Friend

Night started to fall and 'My Friend' asked me if I was hungry, seeing as we had not eaten in a few **years**. I just looked at him and burst out laughing.

That was the first time I laughed since I died.

We both sat down under the stars on a bench and ate some chips that a guy had left behind him who had been out drinking that night. You know what? They were the nicest chips I had **ever** eaten! I looked at 'My Friend' and remarked how my friend - the one who had found my body - and my sister had done the same thing when they were small many years before. I remember telling both of them how *disgusting* they were. Now, there I was - eating a drunk man's leftover bag of chips! We both laughed aloud about that.

Next thing I knew, I was standing in front of my partner, my friend, and my sister. They were at the hospital. I asked 'My Friend' what was going on, and he told me my sister had fallen ill and was going through a hard time. She had nearly died a couple of days before we got there.

Hello, My Friend

I looked at him and said, "*I do not want her to die. It is too soon for her. She is too young.*" I walked over to her bed and reached out to touch her face. I started to remember how close we were as children and the love we had for one another. I rubbed her face. I asked him if there was **any** way I could communicate with her. I needed to help her get better. He lowered his head and said, "*Sadly, she cannot see you in the world she lives in, but you can visit her in a dream tonight - if you wish.*" I agreed straight away. That night, I spent time with my sister in a dream. She awoke the next morning a different person and on the mend, having spent time with me.

When the dream was over, I left my sister and found myself in **another** dream. This time, it was my friend - the one who found me after I died. She was standing outside a hotel in our hometown and I was across the road outside of a chip shop. I got excited and called out to her. She saw me and, with just as much excitement, shouted over to me. As she was making her way across the road, she was nearly run over by a bus, but I put up my hand to tell her to stop in her tracks so the bus could pass her without knocking her down.

Hello, My Friend

I found out later that about six months after I died, she *purposely* drove into a bus in an attempt to kill herself, as such was the mental trauma she suffered after finding my body.

She approached me and we began to talk. I told her I was okay and that there was a 'Hugging Room' in the next realm where a person can go to get a hug if they needed one - which, of course, she found funny. We both found it funny, as I was never really a touchy-feely person while on Earth. The noise around us got very loud, to the point we could not hear each other. I grabbed her hand and asked her to come with me. Amazingly enough, we both began to fly. She remarked how we were like Peter Pan and Wendy - and you know what? When I was alive, we **were** just like Peter Pan and Wendy, as we never really grew up.

Eventually, we reached the field I had been in earlier with 'My Friend' - the field where the children were playing. We landed on our feet with a thud, but just as we did, I was gone. That field was where she and I had first played together as children when she was nine years old and I was seven. I could hear her calling my name, wondering where I had gone.

Hello, My Friend

I asked 'My Friend' why I had to leave her in the dream so abruptly without being able to say 'goodbye'. He replied, "*You took her back to the very field where your friendship began as children. The reason why there was no 'goodbye' is because it is not the end for the two of you. You will see each other again, and even though she is bewildered right now as to why you have left so suddenly, she will figure out what I have said to you on her own when you see each other again. At this moment, life is not too good for her. She is going through a lot with her sons and things are hard. She is still very much affected with losing you, as you were her closest friend - the one she shared everything with - and you helped her with her children. Now, she feels very alone, but she will be okay in time because another childhood friend who you have in common is around her. Their friendship is going to strengthen to a degree of a bond…something like the two of you had. The dream she just had of you is going to help her a lot.*"

My heart sank. She was very close to me - like a sister. We were always there for each other through **everything**. Now, there she was…feeling alone and broken after my death. I was not there for her.

Hello, My Friend

In the blink of an eye, I was in yet **another** dream. This time, it was my partner's dream. She looked pregnant. She was asking me what we should name the baby. For some reason, I said to her, *"We will name him 'Isaac'."* She agreed, and we were both happy with that name. I asked 'My Friend' what did the name mean, and he said to me, *"The meaning of that name is 'Laughter'. You shall laugh again."* It was like I was in her dream to tell her that in time, she will smile again.

• • • • •

Hello, My Friend

Now, all of that seemed "nice to know", but the reality of it all was that by taking my own life, I had redirected everyone else's lives into directions their lives might not have taken had I still been around.

How I wish I had reached out to someone and told them the truth about how I was feeling.

How I wish I had gotten the help that is there through a loved-one or professional...

'My Friend' and I spent some time visiting old areas and places I would have been while I was alive. Seeing some old faces made me a bit lonely. I wanted **so** much to interact with them, but I couldn't.

Hello, My Friend

I started to get angry when I asked 'My Friend', *"Is this it for me? Is this my punishment; to wander the Earth for all of eternity, carrying the regret of what I have done to everyone - including myself? I have had enough! I cannot bear it any longer! I am sorry for what I've done and want to go back - back to that night and **NOT** do what I've done. I want to call up everyone and tell them how much I love them. I want to sit at my children's birthday parties and sing while they blow out their candles. I want to reach out for help from my partner, family, friends, and relevant services. I want to feel the rain on my face again. I want the wind in my hair. I want the touch of my partner and children. I want to laugh with all of them again. I can see **NOW** that suicide is not the answer. Oh, please, 'My Friend': Do something for me!* **HELP ME! HELP ME!**"

I faintly repeated "*Help me*" once more as I fell to my knees, crying from my very heart with the knowledge that no matter **how** much I apologized or cried out for help, I was *never* going back. That broke me more than **anything** ever had in my entire lifetime on Earth.

Then, I heard someone from behind me begin to laugh. I turned around to see a man standing there laughing at me.

Hello, My Friend

I asked 'My Friend' who he was, and he replied, *"Him? Oh, never mind him. He is a liar and a thief who is out to rob, kill, and destroy. He is the one who whispers in the ears of people that they are no good and makes them believe they are worthless or that no one loves or could **EVER** love them - when that is far from the truth. He is the one who whispered in **your** ear that fateful night you died. He filled your thoughts with lies, but don't worry: His day is coming soon - very soon! Do not even look at him."*

At this point, 'My Friend' was at a potter's wheel molding a vessel of some sort. I asked him why he was doing so at a time like this, and he asked, *"Are you finished with the self-pity? Have you cried enough tears? Or shall I continue with what I am doing and give you some more time?"*

I looked at him sternly and said, **"I cannot believe what you just said to me! Can't you see I am completely broken?"**

Hello, My Friend

He replied, "*I thought you were completely broken the night you took your life! So, **NOW** you realize you were **NOT** actually **COMPLETELY** broken, but rather at a place in life where things were getting on top of you and you needed to reach out for help. Going through what you are right now and knowing you cannot turn back time has shown you that in reality, your emotions **WERE** repairable. Now you know you could have been happy again had you reached out. Is that what you are trying to say to me?*"

Slowly, I said, "*Yes. I suppose that is **exactly** what I am trying to say, but I had no words. You have explained it better to me - better than I ever could have to myself. Anyway, 'My Friend', I want to know your **real** name. After spending all of this time together, I think you at least owe me **that** much. And what are you **DOING** at that potter's wheel? Making a stupid vessel of some sort?*"

Hello, My Friend

He said, "*Well, to answer your second question first: This 'stupid vessel' (as you referred to it) is actually - in a strange way - like* **YOU**. *It started out as a teacup, but as a teacup, it could not hold what was put into it. It cracked and broke, so I am now making it into a large vase that can hold a lot more than a teacup can. I am thickening its surroundings in a way that it will not smash, but rather it will smash anything that it hits or falls onto - unlike a teacup that will break at the first fall. This wheel is molding you into something that can help others. You see, I had a plan for you and your life. The night you died, it was taken away. Now, I have to make something new out of you and repair what is left…and I will.*"

I did not understand what he was saying. In fact, I thought he had gone mad with all that kind of talk, so I said to him, "*'My Friend', I think you have finally lost the plot. Anyone would think you were saying you are God!*"

With those words released from my mouth, he asked, "*What was the first question you asked me again?*" I answered, "*I asked what was your* **REAL** *name.*"

He looked me straight in the eyes and said, "*I have not lost the plot, my son. I am who you say I am.*"

Hello, My Friend

I could not believe what I heard! I said to him, *"You are the homeless man who has lived in my hometown for many years. I passed you nearly every day. How could **YOU** be **GOD**?"*

He replied, *"Most people walk past me every day without a second glance. They walk past me as I sit outside of churches they enter in order to try to find me, and I am right under their noses. They ignore me when I sit as the single parent, alone and scared in a rundown flat or as a child who is hurting with no one to love them. They turn their backs on me when I'm a prisoner who everyone has forgotten about and never visits. I am that patient in a hospital bed with no family and an elderly person living alone. I could go on and on with the many disguises I have appeared to people on Earth. I mean, I even went there as **MYSELF**, and they crucified me!"*

I started to get really angry at this stage. I thought back to the night I died and shouted at him, **"If you are who you say you are, where were you when I took my own life while all alone in my room? WHERE WERE YOU?"**

*"My child, I was in that phone call you never made to your partner, family, friend, or helpline to tell them how you were really feeling. People are my vessels on Earth. I depend on others' mouths to speak my truth and for their hands to help others in my name. **I was in that call you never made**"*, he said.

Hello, My Friend

I then asked him why I had to endure so much pain when I was on Earth, and He said to me, *"Everyone has their trials and tribulations while on Earth. I even had my own to bear when I dwelt there."*

I said, *"But it was all too much for me to bear in the end. I couldn't take it and just gave up."* I repeated that with such brokenness:

"I JUST GAVE UP!"

'My Friend' put his arms around me and said, *"You are with me now, even though it is not what I had planned for you. I wanted you to live many more years and see your days out to the natural end I had laid up for you. Nonetheless, we will work with what we have now."*

Hello, My Friend

I suddenly had a thought and said to him, "*Lord, if you may, can I please share my story with others who may be hurting right now and cannot see a way out? Those who may be considering taking their own lives? Can I tell them there is hope in their futures if they just hold on for another day and live in the moment - like you taught me in the playground while watching the children play? Can I tell them that those people in their lives who they think do not love them actually **DO** love them dearly - like I saw in the eyes of my family and friends that day at the cemetery? Can I tell them when they feel alone, they are not alone - that you are in the phone call they can make to a family member, friend, or helpline - like you have told me here this day? Can I tell them that it is okay to reach out for help, as it is a sign of strength and courage - not a weakness like they might believe? Can I tell my partner, children, family, and friends that I love all of them so much and am sorry for the hurt and pain my death has caused? Can I take them step-by-step through this journey I have gone on with you so they can see for themselves that suicide is **NOT** the answer? Please, Lord: I will not ask you for another thing if you allow me to tell all of this to others!*"

'My Friend' looked at me, smiled, and said, "*My child: You already have.*"

• • • • •

Hello, My Friend

Conclusion by the "Homeless Man"

By now, you are aware of who I *really* am. I want you to know that whoever you are right now and no matter how you may be feeling, **you are not alone.** I know life may have set you back. I know people may have hurt you and let you down. Your story may be very different from the one you just read. You may be feeling rejected by someone *right now*...a girlfriend, boyfriend, family, or friends - but sometimes in life, rejection is sent to you not to destroy you, but rather to redirect you onto a much better path, one you would never have taken if those rejections had not come your way and certain people remained in your life.

Some people who are causing you hardship and pain are sent to help build character in you. Even though you cannot understand **all** you are going through right now, if you stick with it, you will be the one to come out on top.

I can promise you that.

Hello, My Friend

In your pain, you cannot see what *purpose* your life has on this Earth, but I can guarantee you that just like the young man in this story discovered, you, too, have impacted others' lives in a positive way. Losing you would be **devastating** for them. Look deep within yourself and remember a time when you were at your happiest and healthiest…a time when you didn't have many cares in the world.

Hold that thought for a few seconds…

I bet you are smiling or you have tears falling, longing for those times again.

Pay attention to this closely: You can and *WILL* smile again if you give yourself the chance to recover and heal. You see, time has a way of helping us heal. As hard as that may be for you to believe right now, I **promise** you it is true. If you hold on and reach out to a family member, partner, friend, or a helpline, you **will** receive the help and guidance you need.

If you are sitting there right now thinking, *"I have no one who cares. I have no one to talk to"*, well, that is not true because all you have to do is call **ME!** Yes, I know you are wondering how you will go about doing that, and I am going to tell you:

Hello, My Friend

Just close your eyes and repeat after me. "*Hello, My Friend...*" and continue talking to me as if I am sitting there with you **right now** - because I am, even though you cannot see me. I will be there to give you the strength and courage you need to pick up your phone and ring the right person or services for you. You have a chance to turn it **all** around.

I believe in you, even if others don't.

All my love,

Your Forever Friend...

~ GOD ~

P.S. If you are wondering what became of the young man in this story, he is with me for all of eternity. His wish is for whoever reads his story to **NOT** make the decision he did that fateful night, but to reach out for the help that is available. Live to see another day and the beautiful life that awaits you!

• • • • •

Hello, My Friend

Support Services in Clonmel, County Tipperary, Ireland

For **anyone** who may have been affected by suicide or who may need **immediate** help, the following services are available within the Clonmel, County Tipperary area, Ireland:

Dan Connolly of **"Taxi Watch Clonmel"** can be contacted 24/7 on **083 8171515**.

June Looby, Jacinta Mullins, Pamela Hallahan, Adam Maber, and John Joe Treacy of **"River Suir Suicide Patrol"** can be contacted on **083 8635386**, also 24/7. This group of volunteers patrols the 'River Suir' Clonmel *every* Friday, Saturday, and Sunday night.

All of the above listed services are private and confidential.

I would personally like to commend and thank Dan Connolly and **all** the volunteers of "River Suir Suicide Patrol" for the excellent, non-judgmental, and life-saving services they provide in our hometown.

Hello, My Friend

For anyone else nationwide or outside of Ireland, you can easily access **Suicide Awareness Groups and Helplines** within your vicinity both online or by ringing the relevant Emergency Services numbers for your areas.

www.ingramcontent.com/pod-product-compliance
Lightning Source LLC
Chambersburg PA
CBHW071544080526
44588CB00011B/1791